When someone asks who you are, you might answer with your name, or with something you like to do ("I'm a ballerina!"), or even by mentioning a relationship ("I'm a big brother!").

The אָבוֹת is the first blessing of the Amidah—a group of blessings at the heart of every prayer service. It asks God to recognize us as descendants of our ancestors Abraham, Isaac, and Jacob, and it links each of us to the family of Abraham and Sarah. It asks God to watch over us, protect us, and bless us, just as God watched over our ancestors.

In the Avot we recognize that God is mighty, powerful, and awesome, but also loving and protective. You can see this balance in your everyday life, too—your mom might be strict about you doing your homework, but she can also be loving and supportive when she helps you with it and praises you when you do well.

Practice reading the אָבוֹת aloud.

1. בָּרוּךְ אַתָּה יְיָ, אֱלֹהֵינוּ וֵאלֹהֵי אֲבוֹתֵינוּ,

2. אֱלֹהֵי אַבְרָהָם, אֱלֹהֵי יִצְחָק, וֵאלֹהֵי יַעֲקֹב.

3. הָאֵל הַגָּדוֹל, הַגִּבּוֹר, וְהַנּוֹרָא, אֵל עֶלְיוֹן.

4. גּוֹמֵל חֲסָדִים טוֹבִים וְקוֹנֵה הַכֹּל, וְזוֹכֵר חַסְדֵי אָבוֹת,

5. וּמֵבִיא גוֹאֵל לִבְנֵי בְנֵיהֶם, לְמַעַן שְׁמוֹ, בְּאַהֲבָה.

6. מֶלֶךְ עוֹזֵר וּמוֹשִׁיעַ וּמָגֵן.

7. בָּרוּךְ אַתָּה יְיָ, מָגֵן אַבְרָהָם.

Praised are You, Adonai, our God and God of our fathers,
God of Abraham, God of Isaac, and God of Jacob.
The great, mighty, and awesome God, supreme God.
You do acts of loving-kindness and create everything and remember the kindnesses of the fathers,
and You will bring a redeemer to their children's children for the sake of Your name, and in love.
Ruler, Helper, Rescuer, and Shield.
Praised are You, Adonai, Shield of Abraham.

אָבוֹת וְאִמָּהוֹת

When you look at yourself, what do you see? Did you inherit blue eyes from your mom? Or a sense of humor from your grandmother? Or perhaps you're an artist just like your great-grandmother. You are descended from all of these women—and the characteristics they have passed on to you are part of your heritage.

Many congregations now include the אִמָּהוֹת in the Avot blessing. Adding the names of the Imahot links us directly to the matriarchs of the Jewish people—Sarah, Rebecca, Leah and Rachel. Just as we ask God to recognize us as descendants of the patriarchs Abraham, Isaac, and Jacob, we ask God to deal kindly with us because of the goodness of the matriarchs.

Whether the Amidah includes just the names of the Avot or also those of the Imahot, it reminds us that as Jews we have inherited God's favor because of our ancestors' goodness and faith.

Practice reading the אָבוֹת וְאִמָּהוֹת **aloud.**

1. בָּרוּךְ אַתָּה יְיָ, אֱלֹהֵינוּ וֵאלֹהֵי אֲבוֹתֵינוּ וְאִמּוֹתֵינוּ,

2. אֱלֹהֵי אַבְרָהָם, אֱלֹהֵי יִצְחָק, וֵאלֹהֵי יַעֲקֹב, אֱלֹהֵי שָׂרָה,

3. אֱלֹהֵי רִבְקָה, אֱלֹהֵי לֵאָה וְרָחֵל. הָאֵל הַגָּדוֹל, הַגִּבּוֹר,

4. וְהַנּוֹרָא, אֵל עֶלְיוֹן. גּוֹמֵל חֲסָדִים טוֹבִים וְקוֹנֵה הַכֹּל,

5. וְזוֹכֵר חַסְדֵי אָבוֹת וְאִמָּהוֹת, וּמֵבִיא גּוֹאֵל/גְּאֻלָּה לִבְנֵי בְנֵיהֶם,

6. לְמַעַן שְׁמוֹ, בְּאַהֲבָה. מֶלֶךְ עוֹזֵר וּמוֹשִׁיעַ וּמָגֵן.

7. בָּרוּךְ אַתָּה יְיָ, מָגֵן אַבְרָהָם וְעֶזְרַת שָׂרָה.

Praised are You, Adonai, our God and God of our fathers and mothers,
God of Abraham, God of Isaac, and God of Jacob, God of Sarah,
God of Rebecca, God of Leah and Rachel. The great, mighty, and awesome God, supreme God.
You do acts of loving-kindness and create everything and remember the kindnesses of the fathers
and mothers, and You will bring a redeemer/redemption to their children's children
for the sake of Your name, and in love. Ruler, Helper, Rescuer, and Shield.
Praised are You, Adonai, Shield of Abraham and Help of Sarah.

PRAYER VARIATIONS

Some congregations pray for God to bring a redeemer (גּוֹאֵל)—the Messiah—who will bring peace to the world, while other congregations pray for redemption (גְּאֻלָּה)—a state of peace and perfection in the world. But *all* Jews are alike in praying for a better and more peaceful world.

2

SEARCH AND CIRCLE

Circle the Hebrew word that means the same as the English.

fathers	אַבְרָהָם	אָבוֹת	אוֹר
our fathers	אֲבוֹתֵינוּ	אֱלֹהֵינוּ	אַתָּה
God of	יִשְׂרָאֵל	וְאָהַבְתָּ	אֱלֹהֵי

We show love and respect for our mothers, fathers, and grandparents in many ways, including by helping them with chores around the house.

NAME GAME

Connect the Hebrew and English names of the fathers.

Isaac   אַבְרָהָם

Jacob   יִצְחָק

Abraham   יַעֲקֹב

WHO'S MISSING?

Fill in the name of the missing father.

אֱלֹהֵי אַבְרָהָם, אֱלֹהֵי _____ ,
וֵאלֹהֵי יַעֲקֹב.

Now write the name in English. _____

PRAYER DICTIONARY

אָבוֹת
fathers

אֲבוֹתֵינוּ
our fathers

אֱלֹהֵי
God of

אַבְרָהָם
Abraham

יִצְחָק
Isaac

יַעֲקֹב
Jacob

PRAYER DICTIONARY

אִמָהוֹת
mothers

אִמּוֹתֵינוּ
our mothers

אֱלֹהֵי
God of

שָׂרָה
Sarah

רִבְקָה
Rebecca

לֵאָה
Leah

רָחֵל
Rachel

SEARCH AND CIRCLE

Circle the Hebrew word that means the same as the English.

mothers	הָאֲדָמָה	אִמָהוֹת	אֱמֶת
our mothers	הָאָרֶץ	אֵלִיָהוּ	אִמּוֹתֵינוּ
God of	אֱלֹהֵי	אַבְרָהָם	אָרוֹן

NAME GAME

Connect the Hebrew and English names of the mothers.

Leah   שָׂרָה

Sarah   רִבְקָה

Rachel   לֵאָה

Rebecca   רָחֵל

WHO'S MISSING?

Fill in the names of the missing mothers.

אֱלֹהֵי _____ , אֱלֹהֵי רִבְקָה, אֱלֹהֵי

לֵאָה וְ _____

Now write the names in English.

_____   _____

4

IN THE SYNAGOGUE

אָבוֹת ◀

גְּבוּרוֹת

קְדוּשָׁה

קְדוּשַׁת הַיּוֹם

עֲבוֹדָה

הוֹדָאָה

בִּרְכַּת שָׁלוֹם

אָבוֹת is the first blessing in a very old and very important group of blessings called the עֲמִידָה. The עֲמִידָה is the heart or center of every synagogue service.

The עֲמִידָה has many names:

- The Hebrew name עֲמִידָה means "standing." We always stand when we say the עֲמִידָה. It is as if we are standing in front of God.

- It is sometimes called the "Silent Prayer" because many people say it in a very quiet voice. They are talking privately to God.

- Another name is שְׁמוֹנֶה עֶשְׂרֵה (the Hebrew word for "eighteen"). Originally, the עֲמִידָה contained eighteen blessings. Now it consists of nineteen blessings (when it is said on a weekday) or seven blessings (when it is said on Shabbat and holidays). The first three blessings and the last three blessings of every עֲמִידָה are always the same. Only the middle section changes.

- The עֲמִידָה is so important that many congregations simply call it the "Prayer" (תְּפִלָּה).

TRUE OR FALSE

Put a ✔ next to each sentence that is true.

_____ The אָבוֹת refers to our relationship with our ancestors.

_____ The אָבוֹת is the last part of the עֲמִידָה.

_____ The עֲמִידָה is said at every synagogue service.

_____ Another name for the עֲמִידָה is שְׁמוֹנֶה עֶשְׂרֵה.

_____ The עֲמִידָה always contains 18 blessings.

_____ When we say the "Prayer," we are referring to the עֲמִידָה.

5

הַגָּדוֹל

the great

הַגִבּוֹר

the mighty

וְהַנּוֹרָא

and the awesome

עֶלְיוֹן

supreme

חֲסָדִים טוֹבִים

acts of loving-kindness

מֶלֶךְ

ruler

עוֹזֵר

helper

וּמוֹשִׁיעַ

and rescuer

וּמָגֵן

and shield

GOD'S GREATNESS

אָבוֹת lists four words to describe God's greatness.

Write the English meaning for each one.

עֶלְיוֹן	וְהַנּוֹרָא	הַגִבּוֹר	הַגָּדוֹל

In אָבוֹת we see four roles that God plays in the lives of the Jewish people.

Write the English meaning for each one.

וּמָגֵן	וּמוֹשִׁיעַ	עוֹזֵר	מֶלֶךְ

The Amidah is also called the "Standing Prayer." When we say it, we stand respectfully before God.

Prayer Building Blocks

אֱלֹהֵי   "God of"

אֵל   or   אֱלֹהִים   means "God."

אֱלֹהֵי   means "God of."

Why do you think the word אֱלֹהֵי ("God of") is repeated before each name in the אָבוֹת? _____

_____

הַגָּדוֹל, הַגִּבּוֹר, וְהַנּוֹרָא   "the great, the mighty, and the awesome"

הַגָּדוֹל   means "the great."

הַגִּבּוֹר   means "the mighty."

וְהַנּוֹרָא   means "and the awesome."

The prefix הַ means "the."

Complete the following words describing God by adding the prefix "the."

גָּדוֹל _____   גִּבּוֹר _____   וְ _____ נוֹרָא

Why do you think the prayer lists so many different words to describe God's greatness? _____

_____

TORAH CONNECTION

Read this verse from the Torah (Deuteronomy 10:17).

1. כִּי יְיָ אֱלֹהֵיכֶם הוּא אֱלֹהֵי הָאֱלֹהִים

2. וַאֲדֹנֵי הָאֲדֹנִים הָאֵל הַגָּדֹל הַגִּבֹּר וְהַנּוֹרָא

Do you recognize the underlined words?

Underline the same four words as they appear in the following lines from the siddur.

(Hint: Some of the words may look slightly different.)

1. בָּרוּךְ אַתָּה יְיָ, אֱלֹהֵינוּ וֵאלֹהֵי אֲבוֹתֵינוּ,

2. אֱלֹהֵי אַבְרָהָם, אֱלֹהֵי יִצְחָק, וֵאלֹהֵי יַעֲקֹב.

3. הָאֵל הַגָּדוֹל, הַגִּבּוֹר, וְהַנּוֹרָא, אֵל עֶלְיוֹן.

4. גּוֹמֵל חֲסָדִים טוֹבִים וְקוֹנֵה הַכֹּל ...

What is the name of this prayer? _____

Write the English meaning of the words you underlined.

_____

Why do you think the words הָאֵל הַגָּדוֹל הַגִּבּוֹר וְהַנּוֹרָא are written in the Torah and then repeated in the עֲמִידָה?

_____

_____

עֶלְיוֹן "supreme" or "highest"

עֶלְיוֹן means "supreme" or "highest."

The word עַל means "on" or "above."

Underline the Hebrew letters that mean "above" in this word:

עֶלְיוֹן

Why do you think God is called "supreme" or "highest"?

_____

_____

חֲסָדִים טוֹבִים "acts of loving-kindness"

חֲסָדִים means "acts (of loving-kindness)."

טוֹבִים means "good."

In the phrase חֲסָדִים טוֹבִים, the word טוֹבִים helps us know how *good* the acts of loving-kindness are.

Which of the following are חֲסָדִים טוֹבִים? Circle the numbers.

1. Abraham welcomes and cares for strangers.

2. Haman forces the Jews to bow down to him.

3. You take home schoolwork for a sick friend.

4. A store owner gives employment to a needy person.

5. Jacob tricks his father, Isaac, into giving him Esau's blessing.

Add your own example of an act of loving-kindness.

_____

מֶלֶךְ עוֹזֵר וּמוֹשִׁיעַ וּמָגֵן "ruler, helper, and rescuer and shield"

מֶלֶךְ means "king, ruler."

עוֹזֵר means "helper."

וּמוֹשִׁיעַ means "and rescuer."

וּמָגֵן means "and shield."

Write the Hebrew word for "helper." _____

Write the Hebrew word for "and rescuer." _____

Circle the Hebrew word part that means "and" in these two words.

וּמוֹשִׁיעַ וּמָגֵן

Fill in the Hebrew word for "shield" in the blanks.

מֶלֶךְ עוֹזֵר וּמוֹשִׁיעַ וּ _____.

בָּרוּךְ אַתָּה יְיָ, _____ אַבְרָהָם.

Why do you think God is compared to a shield?

_____

An Ethical Echo

An important part of the אָבוֹת blessing is the belief in זְכוּת אָבוֹת—"the merit of the ancestors"—which means that we are favored with God's love and care because of the goodness of our ancestors. We have inherited the gift of God's generosity, kindness, and protection because of their faith and their righteousness.

Think About This!

Do you think that זְכוּת אָבוֹת is enough by itself to grant us God's care and love, or do we also need to *earn* those rewards? What good things have you done, or would you like to do, in your life to become worthy of God's blessings and to someday make your children, grandchildren, and great-grandchildren proud?

FAMILY TREE

Abraham, Isaac, and Jacob are called the אָבוֹת ("fathers") of Judaism. Sarah, Rebecca, Leah, and Rachel are called the אִמָהוֹת ("mothers") of Judaism. They were the first family to believe in one God.

Fill in the missing English names on our ancestors' family tree.

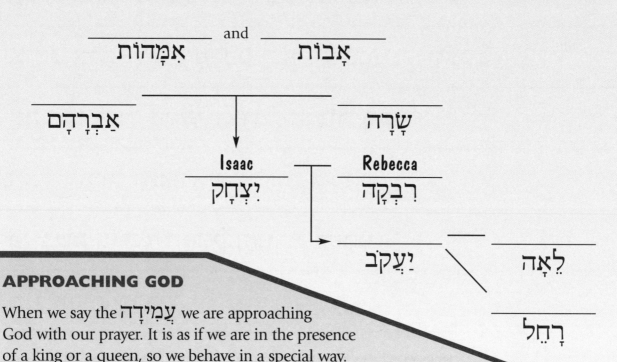

_____ and _____
אִמָהוֹת   אָבוֹת

_____   _____
אַבְרָהָם   שָׂרָה

Isaac   Rebecca
יִצְחָק   רִבְקָה

_____   _____
יַעֲקֹב   לֵאָה

_____
רָחֵל

APPROACHING GOD

When we say the עֲמִידָה we are approaching God with our prayer. It is as if we are in the presence of a king or a queen, so we behave in a special way.

In some synagogues we:
1. Stand.
2. Face toward Jerusalem.
3. Take three small steps forward before we begin.
4. Bow at the beginning of אָבוֹת and at the end of אָבוֹת.
5. Bow several more times during the עֲמִידָה.
6. Don't stop to talk while reading the prayer.
7. Take three small steps backward when we finish the prayer.

How do you think you would feel and behave in front of a king or a queen?

_____

Who is the Ruler we are addressing in the עֲמִידָה? Write your answer in English and in Hebrew.

English: _____   Hebrew: _____

FLUENT READING

Each line below contains a word or phrase you know. Practice reading the lines.

1. עֶזְרַת אֲבוֹתֵינוּ אַתָּה הוּא מֵעוֹלָם, מָגֵן וּמוֹשִׁיעַ.

2. אֱמֶת, אֱלֹהֵי עוֹלָם מַלְכֵּנוּ, צוּר יַעֲקֹב מָגֵן יִשְׁעֵנוּ.

3. אֶת שֵׁם הָאֵל הַמֶּלֶךְ הַגָּדוֹל, הַגִּבּוֹר וְהַנּוֹרָא.

4. הָאֵל הַגָּדוֹל הַגִּבּוֹר, יְיָ צְבָאוֹת שְׁמוֹ.

5. כִּי בְשֵׁם קָדְשְׁךָ הַגָּדוֹל וְהַנּוֹרָא בָּטָחְנוּ.

6. מָגֵן אָבוֹת בִּדְבָרוֹ.

7. עַל הַתּוֹרָה וְעַל הָעֲבוֹדָה וְעַל גְּמִילוּת חֲסָדִים.

8. אָבִינוּ מַלְכֵּנוּ, עֲשֵׂה לְמַעַן שִׁמְךָ הַגָּדוֹל הַגִּבּוֹר וְהַנּוֹרָא.

9. עֹשֶׂה חֶסֶד לַאֲלָפִים.

10. וַאֲנִי, בְּרֹב חַסְדְּךָ אָבוֹא בֵיתֶךָ.

Art st: Ilene Winn-Lederer; Photographs: Terry Kaye (3), Ginny Twersky (6). ISBN 0-87441-758-9 (Avot / Avot V'Imahot); Manufactured in the United States of America.